# I Used to Be Someone…

A collection of poetry
inspired by rural Australia.

By B. T. Campbell

First published by The Rural Publishing Company 2023

Copyright © 2023 Ben Campbell

Print (Paperback): 978-1-923008-02-1
Print (Hardcover): 978-1-923008-03-8
eBook: 978-1-923008-04-5

This work is copyright. Apart from any use permitted under the *Copyright Act 1968*, no part of this publication may be reproduced, stored in a retrieval system or transmitted in any form or by any means, electronic, mechanical, photocopying, recording or otherwise, without the prior written permission of Ben Campbell.

The information in this book is based on the author's experiences and opinions. The author and publisher disclaim responsibility for any adverse consequences, which may result from use of the information contained herein. Permission to use any external content has been sought by the author. Any breaches will be rectified in further editions of the book.

**Cover Design:** The Rural Publishing Company
**Layout and Typesetting**: The Rural Publishing Company

The Rural Publishing Company
Email: hello@theruralpublishingcompany.com.au
Website: https://theruralpublishingcompany.com.au/

# Table of Contents

We Know... ............................................................................. 1

The Point ............................................................................... 4

Steady On ............................................................................. 8

A Letter to Dad .................................................................... 12

One Dollar Eighty-Five ....................................................... 15

The Last Hurdle .................................................................. 19

I Used to Be Someone ........................................................ 22

Footprints in the Dust ........................................................ 25

Until the Ending of the Race ............................................. 27

Midlife Crisis ....................................................................... 29

Perfect Yellow Petals .......................................................... 31

Paternal Instinct ................................................................. 33

Have You Ever? ................................................................... 35

Shifting Sands ..................................................................... 38

The Small Stuff ................................................................... 40

The Critic ............................................................................. 43

The Cross of Stars ............................................................... 46

The Blue Ribbon ................................................................. 49

No Offence...But ................................................................. 53

| | |
|---|---|
| Breathe Deep | 57 |
| Frangipani Sunset | 60 |
| The Distant Star | 62 |
| Too Few… | 63 |
| I Sat Upon a Rock Today | 65 |
| Boots | 67 |
| White, Black and Grey | 69 |
| The Well Runs Dry | 71 |
| The Square of Bronze | 73 |
| I See You | 75 |
| The Quiet Man | 78 |
| Crystal Clarity | 81 |
| Sunlight on the Sea | 84 |
| It Matters | 86 |
| Semi Cooked Bread | 89 |
| Lucky | 91 |
| Dawn | 94 |
| Matriarchal Ode | 96 |
| Badly Wrapped | 98 |
| Our December Days | 101 |
| The Best Mate I Could Ever Have | 105 |
| About the Author | 114 |

## *We Know...*

We've seen it. We've felt it.
We've worn it. We know.
The bounds of humanity,
And how far it will go.
From the torture of loss
And of closure not found,
To the rapture of rain
On a parched, broken ground.

As life it distills us,
Circumstance, it refines;
Til our character's nature
Exposes, builds and defines.

For when others struggle
Some are driven to stand.
As something inside them
Says 'I must lend a hand'.

Though they often stay silent,
These angels of hope,
Their voices sing loudly
To the ones they help cope.
Some never will meet,
With their help never seen.
But it's the nature of mateship
Despite the distance between.

It's understanding humanity.
And it's knowing the score.
It's helping a brother
As an unwritten law.
It's knowing of pain
Like forgiveness withheld;
And it's the love for a sister
An unbreakable weld.

See no one 'has' time
It's a decision you take.
It's the phone call you ignore
and the one that you make.
It's the friend that's lost contact
For the lack of a thought

And the one who's remembered
And actively sought.

Who knows what will happen
What the future will hold
But there is a definite plot line
When the stories are told.
It'll tell of a country
With a generous heart,
That beats for each other
When things fall apart.

And there's an unspoken thank you
And an all knowing nod,
From a worn out old farmer
Who's praying to god.
He can't speak without tremors
Or a recalcitrant tear,
For with the help that's been given
He might just be here next year.

So when it's all over
The divine choirs will grow
For we've touched it, we've been it,
We've lived it, we know.

## The Point

'What's the point?' he said as he knelt in
the dust and cradled the dying calf.
A pointless game of conscience and heart
as he was always too soft by half.
So he picked up the weary, lifeless frame
and carried it back to the truck.
Another useless mouth to feed he thought
as he cursed his rotten luck.

'What's the point?' she said as she stopped at
the dam just a mosaic all cracked and dry
Such a painful, poignant, pitiful thing it is
when the lifeblood decides to die.
So she closed the gate on some more of her
land, just another to add to the score
Unable to stop her heart and mind fighting
and asking if it's worth fighting for.

'What's the point?' he said as he leant on the
shed as the truck drove away from the yard.
The last of the ewes sold for half they were
worth and his heart now indelibly scarred.
The dust and the sweat somehow mixed in his
eyes as he wiped with the back of his hand
His legs seemed to fail the proudest of men
despite how determined he was to stand.

'What's the point?' she said as she sifted the ash
in the place where her dreams used to be.
The twisted black iron and scorched chimney
bricks were all that was left to see.
The smoke in her eyes and the pain in her
heart were surely too much to bare
All she could do was slump to the earth, look
through the black distance and stare.

'What's the point?' he said as he lay on his bed and
looked at the place where she used to lie.
All of his love now a cold space in his life
and the indefinite question of why?
She left without warning, no chance resolution
and nothing but nothing would last
A heart torn apart and a broken man with only
himself and the dreams of the past.

So he made his way to his father's grave near
that of fathers and fathers before.
A practice he did when he needed to think,
to sort things out and be sure.
'There's a point to all this' he thought to
himself as he stared at the marble cross.
No matter what comes and no matter how
hard I will never give in to loss.

As she picked up the flame singed photograph
of their times before struggle and strife
She gathered herself amidst thoughts so dark
and gave thanks she escaped with her life.
'There's a point to all this' she told herself
though her work lay in the ashes beside.
A house may be made of combustible things
but a home is the people inside.

He got back to his feet as a car approached and
put the battered old hat on his head
There was work to do despite circumstance
and the remaining stock to be fed.
'There's a point to all this' he said out aloud as
the sedan finally stopped on the slope
As from the back seats leaped two innocent
hearts with eyes full of nothing but hope.

She answered herself without fear or pause
as she knew that the answer was true
She would fence out the dams and carry the
stuff if that's what she needed to do.
'There's a point to all this' she believed in herself
as she knew she would never give in
When you've come this far you don't back
down until you hear the rain on the tin.

And as the sun started to rest in the western
sky he took some milk to his tiny bull.
Til with a playful bunt and a childish skip
he knew the little fellow was full.
'There's a point to all this - all the blood, sweat
and tears' he knew in his joyous heart
From the ashes, the dust and the painful ends
comes new growth; a beginning; a start.

## *Steady On*

Two young blokes were sinking schooners
In the local country pub.
They'd been there for seven hours,
And had had three lots of grub.
They'd thrown hundreds at the ponies,
And fifties at the dogs.
They'd got themselves in quite a state
Like a couple of yocal flogs.

The barman asked them the occasion;
'The drought is over' came replies.
'Did you not see the rain today?
Did the mud get in your eyes?

Did you not hear the thunder
and the lighting as it cracked?
Just shut up and serve the bloody beer!'
They said; without an ounce of tact.

Sitting quietly in the corner
was a man of country steel.
He raised his eyes to the commotion
To try to gauge these jokers' deal.
He noted they had collars up,
And some yanky cowboy brim
He'd seen their type so many times
And none has bested him.

He walked over to the youngsters,
Slow and quiet as you might.
Then he asked them what the story was
And why they couldn't be polite.
He reminded them of swearing,
With the ladies present here.
And then to keep things pleasant
He bought each of them a beer.

The two young bucks were full of courage
Though primarily of Dutch.
They told him he could bugger off,
But with a phrase of meaning such.
'The drought is over you old bastard,
Can't you see the creek in flood.

We've had a couple of inches
And me boots are caked in mud!'

Now the cockie'd seen a drought or two,
And many floods before.
So he grabbed each rooster by the neck
And showed them to the door.
He looked them right between the eyes
And said 'Now steady on,
To say this drought is over,
Well that's just a bloody con!'

'You know damn well it don't rain grass,
You know it's not done yet.
That you two aren't even from the land
Is my safest ever bet!'
Then he knocked their heads together
And dropped them unconscious on the street.
He turned and straightened up his hat
And returned back to his seat.

The barman met him back there,
With a beer upon the house.
And thanked him quite profusely
For his action and his nouse.
He apologised for the disturbance
And said 'I'm really sorry mate,
But I can't stand the early crow.
It's something I really hate'

'See there are people out there hurting,
And they will for many years.'
He took a sip, and took a breath
As he was fighting back the tears.
'Every time it bloody sprinkles
you hear that it's the end.
And that things are back to normal,
Well it ain't the case my friend.'

'There's so much more to get through
To get back to a place that's right.
And no one crowns the winner
In the middle of the fight.
Don't get me wrong the rain's terrific,
But keep the horse before the cart.
It's like toweling up those bludgers,
...It's just a real good start!'

## *A Letter to Dad*

The dams are all but dry now mate,
The creek is just about the same.
It's all but bloody desert now
With just dust around the frame.
I fed out all the hay you bought;
And we've finished all the grain;
The ration's getting mighty thin
A lot of work and not much gain.

But they say it's getting closer,
As logic says it should.
But I'm losing faith that it remembers
How to be as once it could.
And now they're arguing all about the cause;
Global warming, climate change.
Some say it's just the cycle
If you study the long range.

To be honest I've gone past caring,
Or trying to pin the blame.
I just can't see the point with it
The result is just the same.
Now I'm sure there's things we should've done;
And there's things I know we'll do.
And the only thing I'm glad of Dad
Is that it didn't fall on you.

For it breaks your heart when cattle cry
    From hunger and from thirst.
When we've done all it is that we can do
    And we haven't hit the worst.
And when the sheep hang on the fences
    But it's not their feeding day.
And you bow your head and shed a tear
    And sadly slowly drive away.

We won't give in I'll promise that.
    Though on Mum it's pretty tough.
But you take the hand that's dealt you,
    Even when it's pretty rough.
So I'll beat the sun by one or two,
    To try to get ahead,
To fix the pump, or clean a trough,
    Or do something in the shed

And I know you wish that you could help.
    You'd be here within a snap.
So maybe see if you can find the bloke
    With his hand upon the tap.
    Ask him can we have a bit;
    Maybe even turn it half a turn.
    To help out every one of us
    Before we shrivel up or burn.

The heart it ain't got that much left,
Been broke a time or two before.
But until it gives up beating
We surely will endure.
For someone's always worse-off
Than us and that's for sure.
But thank Christ we aren't competing,
And no one's keeping score.

So old man I'd better leave you now,
And face another day.
It's bloody hard but we're still here,
I guess that's all there is to say.

## *One Dollar Eighty-Five*

Farming is a numbers game,
When you sell and when you buy.
It's the wool cheque when the times are good,
And it's the feed bill when it's dry.
It's insurance, tools and drenches,
Fertiliser, fuel and seed.
It's the price of lamb and mutton,
And for steers back to the feed.
But forget the cents per kilogram,
And even price per ton.
For numbers that make and break your heart
There stands alone but one…

## I Used to Be Someone…

He watched the storm clouds pass him by,
With their broken promises of rain.
As he stopped to pick the mail up,
It was just like yesterday again.
So he threw the bundle next to him,
Just more bills he couldn't pay.
But something caught his eye this time,
Something very different today.
He put the truck back into neutral,
And pulled the letter from the stack.
His weathered hands incongruous
With the hearts and stars across the back.

It's was addressed to him in crayon,
In a little envelope of pink.
And though the 'e' was facing backwards
It had found his armour's chink.
There was no need to open it,
He knew for whence it came.
His niece who meant the world to him
And for her it was the same.
He took the letter from its envelope
With a soft and gentle touch
Though the words were only simple
Their meaning was so much.

And he felt his heart just breaking,
But he also felt it swell with pride,
As he eyes they danced across the words
And the sentiment inside.
It simply said 'I love you',
And 'to help you in the drought'
A gesture so pure and heart felt
From a six year old - no doubt.
As sticky-taped above the words
To help him keep the stock alive
Was all the money from her piggy bank,
....One Dollar, Eighty Five.

She'd been worried how he'd feed the sheep
Now that all the grass was dead.
And all the hay had vanished
From his massive empty shed.
And what would all the cows drink
Now that all the dams were dry
She knew she didn't have the answers
But she also knew she had to try.
So she gathered everything she owned
From the little jar upon her shelf
And she sent it to the ones she loved
More important than herself.

## I Used to Be Someone…

It tore him in an instant,
And then built him back anew.
It added strength to keep him going,
And do what he had to do.
It didn't fix the problems – no,
Some things you can't ignore.
But if a little girl will give her world
He felt he could find some more.
He knew it helped him carry on,
As it filled his bucket up.
If this time had taught him anything
It's you can't pour from empty cup.

So as we battle in the nothingness
And try to count what's lost.
Try to work out what's important
Before you figure out the cost.
Hold on to love and loyalty
And keep focused on the hope.
See perspective's lost so easily,
And it's a steep and slippery slope.
Hold your family close beside you,
And try to keep your dreams alive.
For somewhere in the future
Will be your One Dollar, Eighty Five.

B. T. Campbell

## *The Last Hurdle*

I thought that I'd got through it.
The battle I had won.
But it was at the final hurdle
That it all became undone.
See I dodged beef for all the 90's
No Mad Cow steaks for me.
A sound and solid plan it was,
As I survived the BSE.
And I made my way through Y2K
A tough one you'll remember.
I pulled the plug on all appliances
From December to December.
Then the acronyms return attack
SARS threatened me and you.
So sent my family packing,
And lived alone for all 02.
I thought we'd seen the worst of it,
But we upset the animals again.
This time it was the Budgies,
Who were set to cause us pain.
So in 05 it was all action,
To avoid that nasty flu.
So I let out the pet canary,
And gave away my cockatoo.
In 07 it was again all over,
As one by one the banks were dead.

But I outsmarted Wall Street,
And hid all my money in the bed.
The GFC they called it,
But we had a crisis yet to come.
For it only was about a year,
And the pigs were number one.
So I just became a Muslim,
No eating pork I can account.
And I did really well I think,
As long as bacon doesn't count.
Thankfully we got a break,
For at least a year or three.
But this time it was the real end,
As any Mayan could plainly see.
I didn't think they'd get it wrong,
It was only 5000 years.
So I gave away all my possessions,
And I drank down all my beers.
But worse luck the next day,
I woke up and it was fine.
Except for a raging headache,
And nothing left was mine!
Now I thought I'd reached the bottom.
No lower could we go.
But Ebola scared me half to death.
I'd seen the movie so I know.
Well it was going to eat me.
There was no getting out of that.
So I lived out on a homemade raft,

With just my pluggers and my hat.
While out there in the ocean,
I learned to paddle as a skill.
And I was so bloody good at it,
I made the Olympics in Brazil!
But I guess it wasn't meant to be,
And it crushed this humble Aussie.
My gold medal it was put on ice,
By a bastard Zika mozzie.
Now thankfully I have had some time,
And I'm very glad of that.
But now I'm sure that it's all over,
Thanks to the humble cooked up bat.
So I've taken all precautions,
No handshake from me today.
And I cancelled my standing order,
At the Chinese takeaway.
But I fear it's all for nothing,
And I know it's my time to die.
Coz I just checked my toilet paper
And I've only 7 month's supply!

# *I Used to Be Someone*

I used to think it mattered,
To look someone in the eye.
To offer up a handshake,
Or to say 'until I die'.

I used to hold a word as truth,
And believe it as a bond.
To see the best within humanity,
And not look too far beyond.

I used to stand on principle,
And believe in wrong and right.
To stand up for the little guy
And to back him in a fight.

I used to admire honesty,
And love and hope and trust.
To care for one another,
And to search for what is just.

I used to believe in mateship
Of a promise holding fast.
Friendship through the thick and thin
No matter what had passed.

I used to be that someone
Who would walk out in the rain,
Or feel the sun upon the back
And your childhood again.

I used to be that someone
Who would search the stars at night.
Mesmerised by beauty,
In the absence of the light.

I used to be that someone
Who could stare into a flame.
Transfixed upon the magic,
That no man could ever tame.

I used to be that someone
Who could smell the scent of earth.
And take the time for simple pleasures,
And to recognise their worth.

## I Used to Be Someone…

I used to be that someone,
Who I knew that could endure.
But is that someone, someone else today?
And how can I be sure?

When uncertainty is certain,
And loss is what you've won.
When the battle stands before you,
And the world has come undone.

When you're faced with stark reality,
And there is nowhere left to hide.
When your humanity is naked
And there is no one left to chide.

Don't look to blame another,
There is no fault that counts at all.
Just remember what you're made of,
And answer your own call.

See we all used to be a someone,
And at that someone's core
Are the things that are important
Despite what tomorrow has in store.

For I know that I am someone,
And you are the same as me.
No matter what is thrown our way
There is no need for 'used to be'.

## Footprints in the Dust

The dew has settled early,
As we greet the April dawn.
The pink and purple hues entwine,
In the rapture of the morn.
Today's air is somewhat bolder,
Clean-crisp, and fresh and free.
As we ruminate on sacrifice,
And question what is meant to be.

No parade today, nor ticker tape,
Though in minds their boots go past.
With reverence, respect, and love
In flags that fly half-mast.
Their job is done, now ours takes hold.
With candles held for them.
We must maintain our day of pride,
Not let the years condemn.

For we walk upon a trodden path,
From those who came before.
And the beat it sounds the echo
Of a memory to endure.
Note well the imprint that you leave,
On a life that's held in trust.
Lest we forget, like gentle rain
On their footprints in the dust.

## I Used to Be Someone...

Though age may weary bodies,
Hearts and heads will hold the core.
So our children's children's children
Lose not truth and know the score.
Little feet then march with honour,
In place of those we've lost from sight.
And little hands will pin the medals,
Upon their chest, and proudly right.

So take up a sprig of Rosemary,
And lay down the flower wreath.
Sip quietly on a rum and milk,
For those that rest beneath.
Toss two pennies to the crystal sky,
Fear not the head nor tail.
Salute to those returned not whole,
And those yet to set sail.

In solemn silence; hold as one,
For those who's march is done.
As we thank them for their service,
And for the life so dearly won.
Take heed and heart my cobber.
Hear what that lonely bugle told.
As we stand tall and strong together,
For those who grow not old.

## *Until the Ending of the Race*

The sun still rises every day
In violet, peach and gold.
And it still traces out its daily path,
Like it did in days of old.
Stars still shine as night time falls,
And day gives way to night.
But the sparkling glint is missing now
And nothing feels quite right.

Time has marched by river-like
With determined power-pride.
Oh what we'd do and what we'd give
To stop and turn; reverse the tide.
When a year can pass in just a wink,
And yet a minute feels an age.

The feeling that you're you again,
Is but imposter on the stage.

To move on and keep it going,
Is as tough as you can get.
Like having to remember someone,
That you simply haven't met.
But it's not something to get over,
That's not what you have to do.
Just think and laugh and love and cry
And somehow you get through.

For nothing will replace your time.
No one can take your place.
And as it is it will remain,
Until the ending of the race.
For no rain can wash away your mark.
Nor man or beast erase,
The imprint you left upon the life
Of those you met face to face.

So as sun sinks below horizon,
Melting light into the dark.
The wish is simply simple,
And the resolution stark.
Each day we had is cherished.
No memory blurred by tear.
And love cannot be faded,
No matter what the year.

## *Midlife Crisis*

Some people hit a number,
And then search for magic wand,
To try to fix their happy life,
Or trade brunette in for blonde.
Maybe they buy a sports car,
Or a Harley grabs the eye.
I'm not sure of the success rate,
....maybe it's worth a try.

But now I've heard a little saying,
That for me has struck a chord.
And it's the influence on thinking
And the power of a word.
Now the sentiment's becoming real,
As from truth and time it's torn.
For how old would you really feel,
Without the date when you were born?

Maybe your back, your knee, your hip,
Don't put it down to age.
But to the stories that you've written,
In the lustre of life's page.
Maybe you're not as flexible,
As you were back in your youth.
Just as a mighty oak tree,
Standing proud with roots of truth.

## I Used to Be Someone…

So enjoy each trip around the sun,
Make the most of every pass.
And treasure every minute
On the right side of the grass.
For nought of us can know it,
Be you rich or not a crumb.
Just how many spins you get to make,
And what be your final sum.

So let mistakes give you the wisdom,
And your scars let make you strong.
Your heartbreaks make you tougher,
And fear not you being wrong.
Let your memories be your roadmap,
For the path not figured yet,
And your dreams a destination,
Filled with trial but no regret.

And who's to say what's right or wrong,
Or what'll work for you,
I'm not the man to make the call.
Do what you have to do.
So make a change or keep it all,
Just remember what you've seen.
For it never is too late to be,
Just what you might have been.

## *Perfect Yellow Petals*

I planted them some years ago,
To but remind me every year.
Of the beauty of our sunlit days,
And the times when you were here.

And I watered them sometimes you know,
Not too much but just enough.
And it gave me strength just knowing,
That they're there when times get tough.

And I fed them too quite often,
As I often thought I ought.
Not with that fancy store bought stuff,
But just with heart and with a thought.

And I watched them break the surface,
Just as a small determined shoot.
As it set its sights for sun and stars,
And towards heaven just to boot.

And I watched them set a flower stem,
Then burst with radiant gold.
With their perfect yellow petals,
Like the memories that we hold.

And I watched them fade, then try again,
Like you did within the fight.
Never wanting just to give in,
As a weaker flower might.

And I saw them disappear from me,
And though gone from sight and sound.
They don't stop there, and nor do we,
Until the day our cure is found.

And I felt the cold without them here,
Until sun fell again upon their slope.
To do nought but just remind us,
That in beauty there is hope.

## *Paternal Instinct*

Well he doesn't bat like Bradman,
Though he'll always have a go.
And he never been the biggest bloke,
But he's the toughest man I know.
And he doesn't sound like Elvis,
On account that he can't sing.
And though he can't play like Wally,
Still to me he is the king.

And he's never won the lotto,
Never been that millionaire.
But there is more to life than money,
And that's the crux of it right there.
See for everything he doesn't have,
He's got triple; maybe more.
And as the father of his family
He feels the richest at his core.

If his kids are safe and happy,
He's quite settled with his lot.
But if something ever goes awry,
Well he'll be there like a shot.
And it's not something that he learned to do
Or picked up along the way.
It's called paternal instinct
And it's just in him every day.

See that was who my dad was,
And I bet he's the same as yours.
For all that really matters
Are the ones within your doors.
He didn't care for fancy things,
Or for colour, race or creed.
The only thing he wanted,
Was to be there if you need.

So just take a bit of time out,
Or go and make a cup of tea,
For the man who taught you character,
And how it is you're meant to be.
So shake his hand or hug him,
Do whatever makes him glad.
Have a chat and just be thankful,
For the ones that we call dad.

## *Have You Ever?*

Have you ever scratched rock bottom,
Til your fingers bled to bone?
Have you ever felt a weary heart,
As it solidifies to stone?
Have you ever stood out in the storm,
Yet felt your tears run dry?
Have you ever lost yourself in life,
Just searching for the why?
Have you ever swallowed words inside,
That you simply had to say?
Have you ever worn the black hat,
Because it's easier that way?
Have you ever wished for sunset,

Before the rising of the dawn?
Have you ever seen a kingship slide,
To be but sacrificial pawn?

If you have never been forgotten,
Then please count your lucky stars.
For a man possesses tree rings
In the thickness of his scars.
If you have never sought forgiveness,
Then you are the lucky one.
For one can simply spend a lifetime,
Never knowing what you've done.
If you have never seen the dark before,
Then enjoy your splendid sight.
For its hard to grasp the depth of life,
Without the inverse of the night.
If you have never seen the castle fall,
Then hold on to your sweet power.
For it is hard to watch a pedestal,
Crumble with the ivory tower.

If you have ever stayed in silence,
Though you recognised the pain.
I urge you reconnect the line,
The chance may never come again.
If you have ever closed the door behind,
Then please don't throw away the key.
For nothing is as temporary as
These ups and downs can be.

If you've ever felt that no one hears,
Or cares what you have to say.
Then please just tell me one more time,
Until I hear you're not ok.
If you have ever felt like giving up,
Then see me before you do,
For I might not have been right where you are
But I'll make space and time for you.

## *Shifting Sands*

If your ignorance be bliss my friend,
Then your joy's a stream naive.
That trickles past so shallow,
With but sole intent to leave.

And if all your faith's in castles,
Built with haste on shifting sands.
Then prepare to watch foundations,
Fall through fearful clutching hands.

And if your head's then buried soundly,
In the remnants crumbled there.
Then your eyes are blinded also,
And you can't be less aware.

Though helpless, heartless, hopeless,
Is then the easy stance to take.
The dye is not yet cast my friend,
For it is still your move to make.

So stand upon your own two feet,
And then take stock of where you are.
For if one foot will follow others,
Then you've journeys left afar.

But own the footprints that you've left,
And own the words you've spoke.
Own the love you've given others,
And then own the hearts you've broke.

Let your life not be vicarious,
But made of sweat and blood and tears.
Count up good and bad experience,
Instead of tallying up your years.

And if you find yourself unhappy,
Seeming stuck right where you're at.
Fight off fears perpetuating,
As you are much more than that.

And though weary, flat, exhausted,
May your whole existence feel.
There are forks appearing in your road
And it's you behind the wheel.

And though there is no easy answer,
As is the curse of those alive.
Maybe it's time to not be driven,
But in fact your time to drive.

# *The Small Stuff*

I see you in the small stuff,
That we pass by every day.
In the things we hold so deeply,
And the things we never say.

I see you in the shadows,
And the echoes of the pain.
In the shimmer of the heat haze,
And the coolness of the rain.

I see you in the loamy soil,
In sky, and storm, and cloud.
But most of all I see you
In the wish we aren't allowed.

And though now the dust has settled,
And the brown is back to green.
Somehow the colours lack the lustre,
Of the spring times that we've seen.

See now time seems more impatient,
Where once it was a saint.
Continue on? Well that we must,
But move on that we ain't.

For you exist in everything I have,
Or touch, or hear, or feel.
And I don't want to see that changing,
As any part of any deal.

Despite how hard I fight to hold you,
In that image in my eyes,
I can feel your presence fading,
There isn't such as good goodbyes.

But every choice I make without you,
And each decision I'm allowed.
I can only hope one simple prayer,
And that's I would have made you proud.

If nothing else – it gives perspective,
On our lives led day to day.
And the futility of silence,
When there are words still left to say.

Don't waste the time with one another,
While there is sand left in the glass,
And always choose to opt for kindness,
Despite the colour of the grass.

And when you contemplate the ending,
In the truth we can't surmount
Don't say don't sweat the small stuff,
Just make the small stuff count.

B. T. Campbell

## *The Critic*

He stood before the artwork
Hung upon the pallid wall,
Reflecting years of tribulation
And there painted clear for all.
The palette somewhat limited;
Off-white and faded grey.
Yet it captured subject matter
With all it had to say.
A line or two of darkest black
Like a wrinkle in the fold
Seemed to emphasise the torment
And to somehow make it bold.

He stood entranced by artists work
With but nowhere left to hide
Until the image changed before his eyes
As she came and stood beside.
At first he hardly noticed,
But for shades of green, and maybe blue,
But the more they stared together
The more the picture changed anew.
The grey had faded out of sight,
And the black diminished too
Replace by red and yellow,
And a seeming pinkish hue.

Now commotion drew attention;
It appeared no ordinary event.
And when the children saw the picture
It had changed to heaven sent.
A rainbow burst of colour,
Filled the glass from frame to frame
And the artist gained new plaudits
And a never ending fame.
The rapid change amazing,
Yet somehow quite overdue.
Like a dream that's coming back to life,
And somehow coming true.

It was but just perspective,
With bits just added to the whole.
But the image gained a fullness
And what some may say its soul.
The vibrant firework of children,
Mixed with depth of heart and love,
Took this most ordinary of pictures
And raised it up above.
A masterpiece of timing,
Insight, trust and touch and feel.
Made a priceless family portrait
That evolves and becomes real.

So when you become the critic,
And you evaluate your lot.
And when you make your resolutions,
And you count up what is not.
Take note of all the colours,
Hidden there in plainest sight.
For there is a chance you'll miss them
If your field of vision is too tight.
See the brightness left by others,
Reflected there in what they do.
For when you look into the mirror,
Try not to focus just on you.

## *The Cross of Stars*

The crystal stars stand brilliant,
Against the most ebony of sky.
As I lie upon the tender earth,
And to comprehend I try.
For I see love offending other love,
With but ignorance its sword.
And extremes attacking common sense,
In attempt to break accord.

See it's easy to believe oneself,
When you only hear one voice.
And if that voice belongs to you as well,
Well you leave yourself no choice.
You can convince yourself that you are right,
And wrong shares not your thought.

But maybe you know not everything,
In your own limits are you caught?

I know I'm held within my life,
And the experiences I've had.
There are things I hold with pride and joy
And there are things that make me sad.
Now this doesn't make me solely right,
Nor wrong as case may be.
It simply makes me who I am,
And it simply makes me me.

So today I'll feel the sun with pride,
In the land from which I'm born.
And I'll stand on soil that I love,
And greet a glorious golden dawn.
I'll see a country that astounds me,
With a palette rainbow bound.
And a people made of endless heart,
If they allow theirs to be found.

I know I have not lived your life,
I have not walked the path you walk.
But perspective is only useful,
If you will share it as we talk.
So if you feel a different way,
There is no need to argue, scratch and fight.
For truth's not mutually exclusive,
When we don't need to just be right!

## I Used to Be Someone…

I recognise your right to freedom,
In speech and act and thought.
And I'll defend this right unto the death,
Because you know I think I ought.
And I ask but just one thing of you,
As by a means of courtesy,
That what I believe a right for you,
Well you do the same for me.

So when I stare up at our cross of stars,
And I say I'm filled with pride.
It's because I love our country,
With a heart that won't subside.
And although we may always differ,
And may never walk as one.
We can always walk together,
Beneath the radiant golden sun.

## The Blue Ribbon

It rolls around each year you know,
Like a tsunami building up.
The battle for that piece of felt,
Could be a mighty challenge cup.
For weeks and months they're at it,
To have the best there is this year.
See nothing good is ever easy,
It needs blood and sweat and tear.

As you come down of Grevillea hill,
To the old stoic entrance gate,
You find a friendly locals face,
To say 'I wish you well my mate'.
'It's good to see you've got a few'
The volunteers will always say.
And usually from Notty it's a
Heartfelt 'Enjoy your day'.

So you wind in through the horses,
In their thousands it may seem
There for equine competition
For any points the judges deem.
Each a picture of perfection,
Manicured and on track.
Not a hair is ever out of place
On either rider or on hack.

Then you pull up to the sheep shed,
With lambs and rams and ewe.
And try to scope your competition,
It's just something that you do.
A special place this is for me,
Built in honour of my dad.
And this year we're missing Barry too,
And all the times they had.

There's goats and chooks and wool and art,
Each still searching for the best.
Beside the office where the trophies are
At the completion of the test.
Then it's to the main pavilion,
Where the competition's hot.
Who has got a sponge this year
That could rival Grandma Dot?

Bobby's won the vegetables,
Though hundreds may have tried.
And old Ken has got a second,
With a dahlia planted just before he died.
So much to see and look at,
All the sections seem to thrive.
Reflecting time and perseverance,
And a little town alive.

The last stop is to the bird shed,
And it brings yet another tear.
For there's the budgies, finches, parrots,
But if only Kev was here.
And the schools have done a mighty job,
With displays and works of art.
And it's something to be proud of,
As our little town has heart.

Then it's back through sideshow alley,
And the parent's money pit.
Yet with rides and children's smiles though
It somehow seems to fit.
Sit down to watch a wood chop,
As the slivered splinters fly.
And then down to see the bull ride,
And kid yourself you'd like to try.

Then as darkness falls around you,
An eerie silence seems to fall.
Till the sky explodes with colour,
And the wait was worth it all.
For the joy reflected in the eyes,
Of children young and spry.
As they munch down on a Pluto Pup
Makes you think of days gone by.

The tsunami's all but over,
Next year's entries now to plan.
You're going for blue ribbons,
And a champion if you can.
So see you all in In 2022
It's back on again you know.
And there's really nothing like it,
Not like the local country show.

## *No Offence...But*

I may be just a simple man,
With but few strings upon my bow.
And I cannot do quite everything,
And there is a lot I do not know.

Yet I'd like to think I know the score,
And can read things as they stand.
But there is a new wave to the pandemic,
And it's getting out of hand.

See I've crossed paths with a young fellow,
And after the time we spoke,
I'm left somewhat disconcerted,
As he described himself as 'woke'.

## I Used to Be Someone...

He said 'Sir, it's all around us,
If you look it's everywhere!
And the harder that you look for it,
Well the more you will find there.'

Now this seemed to make a certain sense,
To even a simple man like me.
'You mean if I really, really try to,
I'll see what it is I want to see?'

Now he seemed a bit confronted,
By this question that I'd put.
I guess it's not easy to stay hopping mad,
When the boot's on another's foot.

It seemed I'd poked a hornets nest,
Or pulled the plug from a latte dyke.
As what spilled forth from that point on,
Well I'd never seen the like.

He said 'Have you not heard from Greta?
Have you not seen Pepe le' Pew?
Have you not read the words of P.E.T.A?
To name but just a few.

Did not you hear that footballer?
There is no apt moral defence!
And don't start me on that Dr Seuss!
For Sir, I must surely take offence!'

Now he seemed a little riled up,
But he had much more it would appear.
As his indiscriminate aggrievedness,
Had finally found itself an ear.

'And the statues made of Captain Cook!
And that abhorrent cheese's name!
And the thing I heard that someone said!
We must always pin the blame!'

It was then I had to stop him,
And though I'd probably heard enough.
I was worried for this mental state,
That had got him cut up so rough.

It was not that I'd become upset,
Though this seemed the thing to be
He just seemed to lack perspective,
And had no ability to see.

A bit of a human-watermelon,
With a naive and petty side.
A bit greenish on the outside,
and a little red inside.

He had seemed to lose reality,
Or a grip on this as such.
To erase things that we don't seem to like?
To me it seems a little much.

We can't go sanitising history,
As though it fixes a mistake.
Is it not better left to learn from,
As we choose our paths to take?

Don't get me wrong I'll get upset,
When I think our hopes are sunk.
But I promise you next time I do,
It won't be from some cartoon skunk!

See I think we've missed one simple thing,
That seems to have the world perplexed.
Maybe before we try to cancel culture,
We should investigate context?

Well my faith in human nature,
Took a hit and that's for sure.
As there's more serious repercussions
And I really must implore.

For with this new found 'wokeness'
Comes a 'kleptomaniac-event'.
And no cure have they found for it,
And no vaccine did they invent.

Now I fear that I may have given up,
And alas I've been forsook.
For no matter where I seem to search,
I cannot find the fence he took.

## *Breathe Deep*

Breathe deep the cold of April air,
As you await the rays of dawn.
And stand in reverend silence.
Here to honour; not to mourn.

Let the lonely piper fill your ears,
And the snare drum mark the beat.
As they march upon the very streets,
That you tread beneath your feet.

Smell the sweet scent rosemary,
That is pinned upon your chest.
In remembrance of the fallen,
And of all that gave their best.

Hear the decorations jangle faint,
Each and every dearly earned.
For there is part of them that stayed behind
Even when they were returned.

See the shine on shoes reflects the stars,
And the dreams of times before.
Of the ordinary men and women,
As the backbone of the corps.

Take note of gaps within the line,
And the spaces now left bare.
For today they march in heaven,
With their comrades waiting there.

I look down upon my own chest,
See the medals pinned on right.
Belonging to the grandparents,
Who were there within the fight.

I see my father's decorations,
Think of his flag that's folded tight.
As I feel the pride enveloping,
With the first few rays of light.

I come today to honour them,
And all those they served beside.
For their courage, strength and toughness
And their fortitude inside.

The bugle echoes through the park,
For those that grow not old.
On our most sacred day of honour,
For those still standing bold.

No glory did they leave to seek,
Nor did they glory find.
But their triumph still exists today,
In our gratitude of mind.

So breathe deep the joy of freedom's air
At dawn's break; not finished yet.
And stand in reverend silence,
And pray 'Lest we forget.

## *Frangipani Sunset*

If wishes three I had to spend,
As such is said to be.
I'd use them all upon you,
As a thank you just from me.

I'd paint the orb a radiant gold,
As the horizon and it part.
To reflect the love you give to us,
From the purest of heart.

Then as it climbs through crystal sky,
To light the naked earth.
Is the world illuminated,
That you've given us since birth.

The feel of sun upon the back,
And the warmth that sinks right through.
Is all the hugs of childhood,
That we've each received from you.

Then a Frangipani sunset;
The subtle beauty of your soul.
Would overtake the daylight,
And encapsulated you whole.

The ebony then I'd lace with stars:
The brightest diamonds you can get.
To keep memories alive for us,
And for those we won't forget.

And if I had a thousand wishes,
I'd still use them all as such.
To show our appreciation,
So you know you mean so much.

And when wishes are exhausted,
And it comes back to things to say.
My wish for all the mothers,
Is this perfect Mother's Day.

## The Distant Star

Some holes are made that can't be filled,
The rips are there for good.
Some breaks cannot be set with time,
Though try and try we would.
Some days we'd trade tomorrows,
To but replay a yesterday.
Sometimes we fall and crumble,
When there is nothing left to say.

Though it's not something to get over,
We get through but day by day.
And years will pass relentlessly,
As there is no other way.
It is, some say, just what it is,
And passing it will never.
But what is left for us to hold,
Is our memories forever.

But today is not a day to dwell,
Time will fly by just as fast.
So as we carry on without you,
We can but treasure what has passed.
We remember all that made you,
And love everything you are.
As now you watch intently,
From your far-off distant star.

## *Too Few…*

The hourglass runs constant,
Each silent fall; a moment passed.
And there's no pause to hold the flow back,
Nor a way to know it's last.
Time we know will wait for no one,
Inevitable truth we understand.
But what if we could see the memory,
Attached to every grain of sand.
There'd be pain, and hurt and heartbreak,
Scars from friends who turned their back.
There'd be failure, loss and sorrow,
When it's insight that we lack.
But then there's joy, and hope, and triumph,

And love from those who count.
There's success, and gain, and wins we had,
That we hope just might surmount.

Yet within the pile of moments gone,
There's many grains left unattached.
Neither happy-sad a memory held,
Nor with good or bad are matched.
And though we cannot capture every one,
Once passed it is but past.
As is the opportunity for our imprint,
And for us the die to cast.
So let fear not be a barrier,
Nor let waste your time forsake.
For no one speaks with satisfaction,
Of the chance they didn't take.
These are the times to capture now,
Not let run idle through.
Grab hold and make a memory,
For we can only have too few.

B. T. Campbell

## *I Sat Upon a Rock Today*

I sat upon a rock today.
Hard. Alone. Quiet.
Removed from the clamouring cacophony of humanity that is so desperate to be right that we assure ourselves we are.
…From a society so enamoured with the sound we make that all we make is noise. To be added to the din made by every other person who knows themselves to be correct.
…From a band so desperate for a harmonious sound that there can be no harmony. Just noise.
So determined to hear ourselves that there can be no listening. Less understanding.
We talk. We talk at. We talk to. But not with.

I sat upon a rock today.
Hard. Alone. Clear.
Removed from the congealed canvas of humanity that is so desperate to stand out that we blend in.
…From a society so captivated by appearance that all we become is but a myth. To be added to the fantasy of every other person who sees not themselves through other's eyes.
…From the artwork so desperate to be individual that it becomes ubiquitous. A myth.
So determined to see ourselves that there is no vision. Just blindness.
We look. We look at. We look through. But not with.

I sat upon a rock today.
Hard. Alone. Free.
Removed from the collapsing crab-bucket of humanity that is so desperate to climb that we pull each other down.
…From a society so seduced by our rights that there is no responsibility. Or if there is; it belongs to someone else who dares impinge on our existence.
…From the liberty so imperative it becomes our prison. Our right.
So determined to be admired that there is no appreciation. Less honour.
We hold. We hold up. We hold to. But not with.

We sat upon a rock today.
Soft. Together. With.
Entangled in the bustling beauty of humanity that is so desperate to understand that we stand by each other.
…In a society so desirous of us that there is no them. Or if there is; it is temporary and not eternally divisive nor the end.
…In a community so inclusive that no one falls through. Tolerant.
So determined to walk together that there is acceptance. With respect.
With you. With me. With us. With.

## *Boots*

His boots sit by the fire,
Should probably throw them out some day.
But they're like the cape of Superman,
So it's probably not today.

Just like the old hat on the nail,
And the belt still in the drawer.
And the watch that never kept the time,
Still on the table by the door.

They'll never fit quite right again,
Too big for any other man.
So they can just sit and hold the memories,
For the time being is the plan.

## I Used to Be Someone…

Just like the slab we laid in 85,
Initialed there in the cement.
And the fence as straight as arrows,
Up to the old gate that we bent.

And the shed we made together,
When he taught me how to build.
And the well we dug down by the creek,
That never really filled.

Yet the thing that lasts forever,
Is not the concrete, steel or wood.
It's but the time spent with each other,
Not explained but understood.

And I guess it's easier in hindsight,
To appreciate what's past.
And it's but retrospective wisdom,
That reveals itself at last.

But it says don't waste an instant,
And use up every chance you get.
To treasure those you're given,
And cherish those you won't forget.

For though boots can hold your memories,
Now is the time for sure.
Make sure you tell that hero,
They're not made like him no more.

## *White, Black and Grey*

What's it like? I hear you say.
When you wish for night at dawn of day.
When all the colour fades away,
From white, to black, and then to grey.

How does it feel? You want to ask,
To be empty as the empty flask.
To hide yourself behind the mask,
Avoiding time's most wanton task.

What happened when? You want to know,
That makes the hurt and feelings low.
You seemed so strong, resilient though,
What took you away? Where did you go?

So often we have no idea,
Yet feel we know the ones so near.
But speak the truth and make it clear,
We cannot own another's fear.

Nor can we know another's mind,
Or cut away the ties that bind.
In darkness; fact is all are blind,
Yet to this end we're not resigned.

For each of us can add the light,
And stand by those within the fight.
And hold with them with all our might,
Not let them slip away from sight.

It may be tough but still persist,
As the perfect time does not exist.
Make it the first thing on your list,
And don't lament the chance you missed.

If your life's colour disappears,
And you feel you're drowning in your fears.
If you seem to scream and no one hears,
I pray words fall upon your ears.

A thought that simply must be stressed,
A feeling felt but rare expressed.
In a world that never seems to rest,
If but twice we've met; then twice I'm blessed.

## *The Well Runs Dry*

The well ran dry some months ago.
Now you run but on the dust,
Of the fleeting faded promises
And the faith you placed in trust.
And it'd be human just to give it up,
And sure all would understand.
As the mirage of that diamond dream,
Crumbles back into the sand.

Then watch observers standing by,
With the old fair-weather friend.
Just waiting for the back to break,
As you continue just to bend.
See then who stands beside you,
With extended outstretched palms

And take note who stands in silence,
For you need not take their arms.

And it's easy to fly freely,
With a fair wind at your back.
But you have to plumb the depths of strength,
When the sails fall to slack.
And when the arrows and the slings fall hard,
With each a seeming direct line.
If they knock you down some eight times,
Then you must but stand up nine.

Now just imagine for a second,
As we seldom sometimes do.
If the faith we place in others
Was the same you placed in you.
If you trusted you completely,
And believed in all you are.
Instead of seeking it from others
And then adding to the scar.

If you found the strength to just be you,
Not what you think's foretold.
You'd raise your head to face the sun,
Before the daylight finds you old.
There'd be left but one to count on,
When to the winds your fortune's blown.
For the only legs to stand on,
Are the ones you call your own.

B. T. Campbell

## *The Square of Bronze*

The chill of dawn's crisp cleansing air,
And the brilliance of its light.
The smell of lawn cut fresh again,
And spring shower overnight.
Soft drips from poppy petals,
Faded scarlet through to pink.
The simple pleasures of the day,
It makes you stop and makes you think.

The glint of sun on square of bronze;
Stark there on bed of white.
Engraved with nought but bravest names,
Sparks remembrance from sight.
What souls are those behind the names?
That stood fast upon the brink.
Our fallen sons and daughters,
It makes you stop and makes you think.

Their feet once walked the streets we walk,
But time made different road.
These heroes started just as us,
But with honoured courage were bestowed.
Could you answer if your name was called?
Asked to be that vital link.
Could you forego your everything?
It makes you stop and makes you think.

What connection to that name was there?
At home left waiting same.
Dreaming of the face they knew,
And the joy that never came.
They cried the tears we cry today,
Lives changed within a blink.
Their hearts would break the same as ours,
It makes you stop and makes you think.

What thoughts had they before they left?
Alas no chance for them to know.
The place they'll hold for time anon,
As they fell towards the foe.
So for our freedom and our way of life,
Raise a glass and take a drink.
And cast a thought to those not here,
It makes you stop and makes you think.

So stop and take a pause today,
Or go down to Anzac Park.
And think of all the people,
Not just the names upon the plaque.
Pray for the day we add no more,
And from that time our peace to stem.
For as it is for time eternal,
We shall but remember them.

## *I See You*

The clock upon the wall has stopped;
A mirrored wish it seems of yours.
As a wistful breeze creeps gently in,
Through lonely halls and lonely doors.
It dances with but ghosts of joy,
In layered dust upon the floors.
To the silent echo of a broken man,
Stills searching for a cause.

And a black mosaic fills the void,
Of the helpless hardened heart.
As you fight to fit the pieces back,
Tempered as they're torn apart.
Each jagged edge cuts deeply,
A macabre, dark form of art.

## I Used to Be Someone…

Rebuilding ashes into human form,
Is more a question 'if' to start.

And that hollowness inside of you,
The aching, acrid pit.
Consuming hope and happiness,
And your essence bit by bit.
One forward, is but three steps back,
And you feel it's time to quit.
As the crown of pain that now adorns,
Is all that seems to fit.

But hold, I see you in there,
Though just a single ember's glow.
The remnants of the greatest soul,
Is now but fire burning low.
It's oxygen's exhausted,
By the fear to well you know.
So it's time to breathe it's life force back,
One breath; just take it slow.

Now there is no race important,
Nor such a competition just.
And it's hard to find direction,
With a compass full of rust.
So don't rush to find the answers,
Take the time to settle dust.
For though I know that you are in there,
It is only you you need to trust.

If only I could be your lantern,
To illuminate your dark.
Or be the flint to strike upon you,
And to give you back a spark.
And I see that struggle drowning you,
If only I could be your ark.
And though I see you're lost within yourself,
I will hold here; a constant mark.

As I've always been beside you,
I promise that I'll always be.
For no matter what confronts you,
You'll have certainty in me.
Hold on my friend I see you.
Hold on until you're free.
Hold fast till in the mirror,
It's back to you that you can see.

## The Quiet Man

He never took the centre stage,
More to the side and back a bit.
Not through any lack of confidence,
It was just where he chose to fit.
And he never chased the glory,
As it didn't fit the plan.
He just watched and felt the world go by,
As the gentle, quiet man.

But his eyes grew grey and tired,
As over time they'd seen so much.
And the heart he'd given most of,
Now was hardened, scarred and such.
The one who would do anything,
And help in every way he can.
Now but watched; numb, as the world went by;
Just an empty, hollow man.

A sandcastle washed by ocean waves,
He folded back into his crease.
And the nothingness eroded him,
And he left us piece by piece.
His care they took for granted,
And his love no better than.
He vanished just as the world went by;
A forgotten, used up man.

He left little trace behind him,
Except in hearts filled with regret.
And a little note clutched in his palm,
For those who would forget.
The final thoughts and thinking,
Never heard in his lifespan.
Each line gained extra meaning,
Written by the quiet man.

'These are but one man's thoughts' he wrote,
'Of use to you; I can't be sure.
So take note of what you choose to,
And leave the rest here at the door.
For though a book can teach you plenty,
No doubting that it's true.
There's no substitute for love and pain,
And things that you go through.

Yet you have no right to break another,
And worse yet to know you would.
For if you go ahead regardless,
It cannot be misunderstood
For you know that you have made that choice,
To cause another's pain.
And I urge you to question actions,
If you got to make the choice again.

And your handshake must be valued,
But most of all by you.
So when you choose to make a statement,
Back it up with what you do.
For words are nought but hollow breath,
When but orphaned are they cast.
Without the spine of action too,
They are just mist that doesn't last.

Such is a promise without substance,
And a thank you without heart.
To then pledge appreciation
Is just falsehood from the start.
If you then speak of gratitude,
But fail then to act with grace,
You cannot escape the guilt you own,
Set solid in its place.

And don't say you don't have time today,
We have the same each day we spend.
It's you who chose to make priority,
And then on what you do depend.
So when a friend holds you within their heart,
Hold on with all you can.
And don't ever take for granted,
Lest you break the quiet man.'

## *Crystal Clarity*

The rain upon the windowpane,
As entrancing as a dream
Tiny rivulets run freely,
Each but tracing out its stream.
Each drop must find its own path,
From left to right and bend.
Until it finds its final resting place,
And falls to meet its end.

Like a tear that runs from broken eyes,
Finding salty-path across the cheek.
Expressing words unspoken,
And the thoughts that we should speak.
As it comes to rest a moment,

Before its final fated fall.
You see with crystal clarity,
A single drop can say it all.

Yet so much we leave in silence,
Until forced eulogies reveal,
Just what we mean to others,
And the depth the heart can feel.
Still we wait to find the perfect time,
So often never found.
Thus thoughts and feelings so important
Are but buried in the ground.

We assume we're indestructible,
Or that chances will return.
And time's the hardest teacher,
As through experience we learn,
That we dance upon a precipice,
So finite, fragile, fine.
Not knowing where the edge is,
Of either yours or mine.

So tell me your eyes are open,
And that you see me here today.
That you hear the heart that's beating,
And not just the words we say.
Tell me you feel my outstretched hand,
Despite how far it has to go.
For it will always be there for you,
While ever I can make it so.

If my love you have you always will,
For a caring heart is true.
And nothing is more important
Than the importance just of you.
Tell me you understand me,
For when we must answer curtain calls
There can be nothing you could ever doubt,
When that final tear drop falls.

## Sunlight on the Sea

I remember you my friend,
In the days of daisy chain.
With hazel eyes that sparkled,
Like the sunshine through the rain.
Boundless child's dreaming,
Belief's imagination. Hope.
Your world the smallest it would be,
Still limitless in scope.

I remember you my friend,
In our months of in between.
Wide hazel eyes expanding,
With the rapid changing scene.
Foundation bricks of character,
Faith. Loyalty and trust.
Our world accelerating now,
Yet still intertwined and just.

I remember you my friend,
In the years of distant heart.
Of hazel eyes left longing,
Always together; yet apart.
Growing obstacles impinging,
Time and distance. Life.
The world but drifting sailboat,
After anchor severed strife.

I remember you my friend,
In the times of bitter break.
Of hazel eyes left blinded,
By the tears of fortunes' sake.
Aspiration left eroded.
Trust and love. Apparent gone.
The ugly side of human nature,
Push away. Pretend. Move on.

I remember you my friend,
In your hours of giving up.
Of faded eyes exhausted,
As you pour from empty cup.
Your walls now built around you.
Feel not again. Protect.
Care not for consequences,
And thus reality deflect.

I will remember you my friend,
And even if it takes an age.
I'll hold to see that hazel sparkle,
As you dance back on your stage.
You will remember you my friend,
You. The sunlight on the sea.
And as you crest the waves below
But just remember me.

# It Matters

Let not the grey hair fool you,
Nor the wrinkled weathered skin.
For a soldier stands before you,
With beating lion-heart within.
For he'll march while ever he can stand,
When the piper's haunts begin.
To drum beats echoing the past,
In a rank that's growing thin.

Let not his dark eyes fool you,
Nor the blank and vacant stare,
A proud veteran is before you,
Though with heavy cross to bear.
For there's pride in every tear that falls,

And a never ending care.
For today he thinks not of himself,
But of only mates not there.

Let not our flag stop waving,
As the assembly marches by.
And applaud their valiant service,
With that teardrop in your eye.
Our freedom paid for dearly,
With each of them that had to die.
And with nothing but a grateful heart,
Know but for the grace of God go I.

Let not the bugle go unanswered,
As the Last Post does impart.
Just as Reveille calls to action,
That silent moment stirs the heart,
Think what it means to be Australian,
An honour just to be a part,
Of our nation's sovereign future,
With the Anzac as a start.

Let not the digger stand alone today,
In that April early frost.
For he fought for every one of us,
As each battle line he crossed.
With each mate that fell around him,
A very part of him was lost.
As the life that we enjoy today,
Can come not without a cost.

Let not the moment pass you by,
With sprig of rosemary on chest.
Though thank you may not seem enough,
It just might be the best.
Take his hand within the palm of yours,
Look into eyes that stood the test.
And let him know it matters,
As always forget we lest.

## *Semi Cooked Bread*

Cold toast and a cup of Earl Grey tea.
Lukewarm; the way it's meant to be.
From little hands and hearts with glee,
For their greatest friend; a guarantee.
Tired eyes awake and then try to see,
Breakfast in bed; with children three.
With giggles and laughs and smiles free,
For the one they love; deservedly.

But little do her munchkins know,
The things she feels but will not show.
The bond she signed their age ago,
As she lives her life to help them grow.
Her hopes and dreams and fears below,
The doubts she has in her although,
She'd give everything before they go,
For a mother's love you can't outgrow.

A pillar of strength and heart of gold,
She can but write her story as it's told.
With arms to hug and hands to hold,
For painted knees or hearts consoled.
Always there; like a blanket for the cold.
The one and only. The brave and bold.
No matter what's dealt she'll never fold.
No matter the time and no matter how old.

The handmade cards with sentiments read,
The admiration we feel that goes often unsaid,
For the care you have given, the ambitions you fed.
The time that you spent and tears that you've shed.
Guiding the path with each step that is tread,
No matter how far that your family's spread.
Your love is returned from our heart and our head,
If but only in tea cups and semi cooked bread.

## *Lucky*

When you sit amongst the darkness,
In the shadows of this life.
Taking stock of all your battles,
Through the tough and troubled strife.

Looking inward at the blackness,
With the storm impending sky.
Left lost, broken, battered, bleeding,
Doubts how lucky am but I?

And as your body starts to fail,
And the joints refuse to bend.
When your energy begins to fade,
And your youth has met its end.

## I Used to Be Someone…

A quick glance upon the mirror,
Is then met with nought but sigh.
Time's ever present forward march,
Questions how lucky am but I?

And when the teeth of grief bite deeply,
And your heart has been torn out.
When nothing seems to matter now,
And when all that's left is doubt.

When the love you had evaporates,
And you feel the end is nigh.
One last apparent-honest feeling,
Oh how lucky am but I!

But I guess it's all perspective,
When the pushed comes down to shoved.
For before a heart can really break,
First it must have truly loved.

Now a cache of cherished memories,
And although you've said goodbye,
Some people never have the privilege,
So how lucky am but I?

And though the bones may now be weary,
As the years must take their toll.
Just think of where those bones have been,
Not the bit-parts; but the whole.

And though pain and scarred experience,
May bring tears unto the eye.
With everything those eyes have seen,
Just how lucky am but I?

So when the shadows start to lengthen,
As daylight begins to fade.
You can dwell on all the things you've lost,
And just the mistakes you've made.

But when you see the sunrise,
That crack of light through purple sky.
Given chance to recommence once more,
Then how lucky am but I?

## Dawn

If we could only hold the sun back,
To but delay the black of night.
For just a few more hours,
We would hold with all our might.

Maybe then we'd find the strength,
Turn back a day, a month, a year.
To make just one more happy memory,
Instead of one more painful tear.

For just one more conversation,
A cup of tea; or even half.
There is no extent to what we'd give,
For just a hug; a chat; a laugh.

But as dusk gives way to starlight,
The stark reality sinks in.
To illuminate grief's futile wish,
Sprung just from pain within.

The naivety to fight with time,
Though desire may shoot true.
As we turn to face the future,
And think of precious times with you.

As the tears clear from our aching eyes,
We can now muster just a smile.
To know you're home; at peace at last,
Free from every earthly trial.

So when the first few rays of new day's light,
Trace the paths of absent friends
We can but hold with one another,
As time heals the heart and mends.

We promise never to forget you,
Nor the person that you were.
For if God ever made a trusted ally,
Well that person; you were her.

The defender of the hopeless case,
And that great teacher that we mourn.
Now the light you brought into the world
We must but find in every dawn.

## *Matriarchal Ode*

She must be of diamond,
Cut from a single crystal stone.
The strong and safe foundation,
From where all that's good has grown.
She's tougher than the toughest teak,
And the bravest of the bold
Adored and irreplaceable,
With a heart of pure gold.

Right there from the beginning,
No hint of wavered strength.
With warmth that knows no boundary,
And patience without length.
She always goes that extra mile,
No limit what she'd do.

And each and every tear you've shed,
She cried them with you too.

The glue that holds the family,
The one who always stays.
The love that never fades away,
To the end of all our days.
We know that it will come and go,
Possession, property and things.
But nothing can or will compare,
To the loyalty she brings.

And we know it's not been easy,
No cakewalk every day.
To give more than ever given,
Is not an easy role to play.
But change it she would never,
Not even if she could.
Coz she's always had that little knack,
To turn the bad things into good.

So wherever it is you are today,
And wherever she may be.
If you can hold her in your arms
Or if she's gone from what you see.
Know a thousand thousand thousand words,
Can not describe the sum.
Of the love we feel for everyone,
That's ever been called mum.

## *Badly Wrapped*

Rough fingers cracked and calloused;
Black-oil, diesel stained.
Search out tape and kitchen scissors,
Where last year's paper's self-contained.
A card of wisemen three in score,
Envelope a little tight.
With Rudolf on the left edge,
And Santa Claus upon the right.
Printed words; of course a cliche,
But written thoughts not so.
Inscribed in time with halting pen,
An entire heart on show.
Finished with 'love always',
A faint x or two to end.
The most sincere of messages,
That a man could ever send.

The present then sat pride of place,
A box; eight inches long.
With three feet of gold-star paper,
Just so nothing could go wrong.
The faces neat as brand new pin,
Fixed down and looking tight.
But the ends were not so easy,
With folded edges not quite right.
So four laps around with sticky tape,

A yellow ribbon roughly tied.
A trim, a tuck, a curl and card,
All just evidence he tried.
Placed then amongst the others,
Beneath needles green of pine.
With ornaments and baubles,
Where lights and tinsel intertwine.

Then one by one they vanished,
Replaced by smile as were claimed.
Until when lights were finally turned off,
Only one small box remained.
With a hardened heart and fingers,
And a grief that loss has taught,
He placed the box back in its lonely drawer.
Maybe all that counts is thought?
A thousand dog-eared memories,
He then stumbled through in mind.
Of the happiest he ever was,
And would ever be resigned.
They say don't cry when it is over;
But smile for it was.
Yet the truth is somewhere in between,
In existence just because.

So my wish is Merry Christmas,
To you and all of yours.
Be they neat in golden paper,
Or forgotten in the drawers
Be they standing right beside you,
Or just a thought in small amounts.
As there's a preciousness in thinking,
And it may be all that counts.
Just a simple thought in substance,
Yet proverbial in fact,
For both man and little boxes,
There is a science not exact.
With a truth so oft neglected
Yet veracity so apt.
Some of the greatest ever gifts in life,
Are the ones come badly wrapped.

## Our December Days

The show it may be over,
As shot and colour fades away.
The Champagne corks now lay redundant,
Like the plans of yesterday.

And as our vessel's finally emptied,
To refrain of 'Auld lang syne',
There's a thought of simple gratitude,
For all those who've filled up mine.

For when the colours burst above us,
To end our own December days.
Tell me your cup has runneth over,
With all the memories that amaze.

## I Used to Be Someone…

For some things it's but a chapter,
Just turn over; write some more.
But sometimes the story's over,
And there is nothing left in store.

So as we close our eyes to darkness,
With only faith that we'll awake.
We can but pray to land in positives
On the scale of give and take.

And when our road has finally ended,
As all roads must sometime do.
These a promise that I make right now,
As an oath I swear to you.

For at the point at which I leave you,
Where so ever that may be.
I shall take a thought and plant it,
So there may grow a mighty tree.

And though I may never see it grow,
Nor take refuge in its shade.
There is comfort in just knowing,
A grace that is of friendship made.

And when time it comes upon you,
To sit beneath the branch and leaf.
There is but one wish that I make for you,
And one solitary belief.

For whatever has befallen us,
And whatever's gone before.
Whatever trials we've had to face,
There is but one thing left for sure.

From root to trunk to tip of crown,
In scale of vastness scope,
I pray that you reap the richness,
From a seed of endless hope.

## The Best Mate I Could Ever Have

Desmond Henry Albert Campbell.
Born in 1949.
And now to eulogise the man,
Well, the honour it is mine.

For those who haven't met me,
My name is Ben; his son.
And I hope I can do him justice,
When all is said and done.

It may seem strange to rhyme the thing,
But I need to make it flow,
And it's the only way that I can keep,
My tears and heart in toe.

In '73 he married mum,
The apple of his eye.
And we thank God today because,
Their love can never die.

In '78 there came a change,
Named Sal, a lovely girl.
And I guess looking for improvement,
They had another whirl.

With luck it was successful,
And they had another kid.
And we never went without a thing,
Though I know he sometimes did.

See he lost his Dad when just a boy,
And then a farm he had to run.
And it's a daunting proposition,
When you're not even twenty-one.

But that he did from that day on,
Right up until last week.
Through fire, flood and famine,
Not a fortune did he seek.

He did it for his family,
To make sure we got through.
And Dad, everything that we have now,
Well that's thanks to Mum and you.

He cherished being Uncle Des.
And he so loved just being Pa.
And for Zoe, Tom and Harry
Well, he was just a star.

Dad did his national service,
When Vietnam it was at war.
All the time whilst farming,
And keeping wolves from every door.

And he shore his share of woolly sheep,
With the handpiece as his tool.
And then he built the Ag plot
At Gulgong's local school.

Now here he was a legend.
For he seemed to have a special way.
With the rogues and naughty children,
Who with him were sent to spend the day.

Now if you will indulge me,
I have some stories just for you.
Of the things he found along the way,
And things he loved to do.

There are a couple of facts in here,
And myths that I'll correct.
But firstly, let me start
With his love of Global Shop Direct.

My Dad he loved a gadget.
If it was cheap and it was good.
But why we need 18 Shamwows?
That I never understood.

But his ladder is quite useful,
And the knife sharpener does its deed.
He loved to watch the infomercials,
Because you don't know what you'll need.

## I Used to Be Someone…

But rarely was he happier,
When in Dubbo did he find,
An outlet store with everything,
Well…of the Demtel kind.

Now he also loved tomato sauce.
But it was a source of consternation,
And not because he liked the stuff,
More it's liberal application.

He'd have it on a pie and chips,
Well as everybody should.
But on Weetbix in the morning?
You know I'm pretty sure he would.

And Tom Sauce for a sandwich,
And I won't tell a lie.
On ice cream for dessert?
I can't confirm but can't deny.

His love of old tomato sauce
Was well known and that's for sure.
He got 4 litres as a wedding present
From his brand new mum in law.

Dad was known for many things,
He could snore amongst the best.
On one trip to Sydney I slept in the bathtub,
To try to get some rest.

We never had him measured.
He was not quite a jumbo jet.
More a jackhammer chainsaw
That wasn't serviced yet.

For more than a quarter century
He called the RSL his second home.
From its workers and its patrons
His thoughts would seldom roam.

You see he loved this little town of ours,
From the moment he was born.
And there's a hole in Gulgong's fabric,
Now that he is gone.

He loved his time in Apex,
Serving the community with mates.
And he played and coached the Terriers,
As a bloody good five-eighth.

He did everything to help our town.
Absolutely anything he could.
If there was a cause to help,
Well help it that he would.

He ran the P&C at school,
His normal Tuesday date.
And for longer than he should have
He ran Border Leicesters for the state.

See Dad really loved a meeting.
Which generally he chairs.
And I'm not sure how God works it,
Or how he runs upstairs.

But I bet within a week or two,
With his newfound resident,
There will be another AGM,
To make Dad the President.

For over forty years he ran a sheep stud,
And he really loved the shows.
And as a judge and steward,
He earned respect for what he knows.

He earned respect for what he's given,
And was admired for what he's done,
And the people he met along the way,
He loved each and every one.

A champion of champions
At the Sydney Royal Easter Show.
And just a bloody legend
To anyone who'd know.

He loved animals with all his heart,
His dogs and cattle herds.
And he loved his Border Leicesters,
And he really loved his birds.

We always had a cocky,
And even once an old emu.
All so we could have the Coat of Arms,
He found us a kangaroo.

But what really was his pride and joy,
That we cared for day and night.
Probably his crowning glory,
Are his peacocks that are white.

Though he never got to sell one,
He would have one where he's at.
They'll always be there at Avoca,
Dad. I'll guarantee you that.

I know he will always be there with me.
With every step and stride.
And when I think about him,
I will think of him with pride.

When I go past the High School Gym,
And see their grass that he helped grow,
Or when I hold sheep for him
In the shed at Gulgong Show.

He worked so hard to get them.
Without him they just wouldn't be.
And that's just what is tangible,
There's so much more you never see.

So thank you all for being here.
And when you think of times you had,
Know whatever it is he meant to you,
You meant much more to Dad.

He thought of everyone as family.
No matter colour, race or creed.
And he thought of everyone as equal,
If you fail or succeed.

He taught me everyone is worth your time,
Despite how busy you may be.
And your shoulders there for anyone,
When it's grief or trouble that you see.

For a man to touch so many
With his love an inner peace,
I know that Des's legend
Will grow and never cease.

He fought bravely just to stay here,
But went peacefully on his way.
And if only we could go forever
Because there is always more to say.

He was the best mate I could ever have
So I try not to be sad.
And he also was my hero
But most of all my Dad.

...for Des

## About the Author

### B. T. Campbell

B. T. Campbell is a fifth-generation farmer and grazier who grew up on his family's sheep and cattle property 'Avoca' in Gulgong, Central Western NSW.

After a distinguished career in Education as an English and Drama teacher, Ben retired from his Head Teacher position. He returned to the farm full time in order to help his family navigate the severe drought that ravaged the Australian countryside from 2016 through to 2020.

After his father's passing in 2019 Ben assumed the pivotal managing position for the family's stud and commercial stock enterprises, where he currently works as the principal of Avoca Stud Stock.

With a unique breadth of lived experience, Ben communicates the vast scope of the human condition with an authority and sensitivity that allows readers to engage on a very personal level with his works.

As a celebrated playwright, author, and poet Ben's collection of work; *I used to be someone,* is bound to be the first of many experiential journeys for his audience.

www.ingramcontent.com/pod-product-compliance
Lightning Source LLC
Chambersburg PA
CBHW040159100526
44590CB00001B/6